COLORADO WILD FLOWERS

FOREWORD

The generous acceptance of previous printings of *Colorado Wild Flowers,* first published May 30, 1953 under the directorship of Dr. Alfred M. Bailey, has necessitated the present revised edition. The authors, Rhoda and the late Harold Roberts, were enthusiastic nature photographers, and their pictures of Colorado wild flowers were made from the tops of the highest mountains to the low pinon-juniper areas of the state.

This Museum Pictorial (No. 8) was the first publication of the museum to be illustrated in color, and because of its popularity, Museum Pictorial No. 13, *Mountain Wild Flowers of Colorado* by Rhoda Roberts and Dr. Ruth Ashton Nelson was issued July 1, 1957.

Mr. Roberts was a prominent Denver attorney and a long-time Trustee of the Museum. He served as Chairman of the Building Committee for many years and made numerous contributions to the welfare of the Museum.

THE PURPOSE of this booklet is to portray a few of the common wildflowers of Colorado in such form that they may be recognized and their names learned without the use of any botanical key. The color plates here published show fifty different flowering plants, each of which grows in abundance in some part of this state. Most of them are found also in other areas, particularly in the Rocky Mountain states. With the description of each plant, some reference is made to the life zone in which it grows, but no attempt is made to give the geographical extent of its range. In every instance the photograph reproduced was taken on Kodachrome film of a living plant in its natural setting. All of them are shown in full bloom as we see them in Spring or Summer, except milkweed, page 43, and cattail, back cover. These appear in seed as we find them along the roadsides in October.

The flowers are here arranged in substantially the order that the families to which they belong appear in most botany manuals. Some references to these plant families, and to the genera and species into which they are subdivided, will be found on page 57. With each plant we have given the common name most familiar to us. As there is little uniformity in common name usage, others may know them by other names. We have added in each case, in italics, the Latin botanical name, with abbreviated identification of the botanist first using that name. The English form of the family name is also given. We have tried to select flowers representing as many plant families as possible, and among them to cover plants from different altitudes and from different types of soil and growing conditions.

Some of these photographs were taken at close range, with a long focal length lens, to show on a large scale the beauty of very small flowers. Others were taken with different equipment so as to include the form of the complete plant and show plainly its natural setting. In all cases the size of the flower and of the entire plant are given in or may be inferred from the descriptive text. The figures used are approximate, and considerable variation from these sizes will be found. The colors are as accurate as colorfilm and high class press work can make them.

The pictures here reproduced were all taken by the authors between the years 1941-1952. Most of the plants were found within a few hundred feet of some well traveled road. A few of the pictures were taken in adjoining states, but in every such instance the species shown is found in the same sort of environment in Colorado. Many of these flowers are reproduced as part of the setting in habitat life groups in the Denver Museum of Natural History. Look for them there, and also get acquainted with them in their native haunts. They add decided interest to outdoor ramblings.

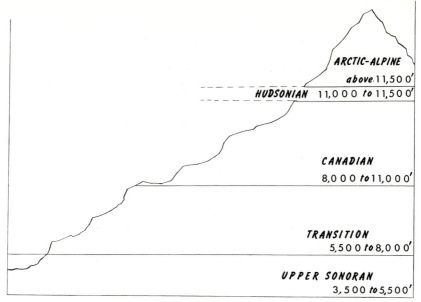

ARCTIC-ALPINE
above 11,500'

HUDSONIAN 11,000 *to* 11,500'

CANADIAN
8,000 *to* 11,000'

TRANSITION
5,500 *to* 8,000'

UPPER SONORAN
3,500 *to* 5,500'

LIFE ZONES

Climate, which is a composite of prevailing temperature, length of season and average moisture, is the chief factor in deciding where plants of any given species can grow and propagate. Soil type also plays a part, and if extremely unfavorable may totally exclude some species of plants from a large and otherwise favorable area, but in general, soil is the minor factor. In Colorado, climate is largely determined by altitude, so here, as we pass from one elevation to another, we find plant life arranged in horizontal layers or zones of the sort illustrated in the above sketch. The thinness of air, in the sense of less oxygen per cubic foot of air, that goes with high elevation, seems in itself to have little effect on plant life, but the prevailing cold, the long period of snow cover, and the increase in annual precipitation, that go with elevation in our mountains, do have a profound influence on plant growth. High latitude has much the same effect as high altitude, so that the timberline conditions we find in Colorado at from 11,000 to 12,000-foot elevations are very similar to those existing at sea level near the Arctic Circle. Growing conditions, and prevailing plant species, at these widely separated places, are, for this reason, much alike.

These zones of life have no sharp boundaries, but tend to intergrade into each other. Many species of plants normally inhabit parts of two or more zones, and local conditions may so influence climate that particular species of plants will be found growing at lower elevations, or at higher, in one part of the state than in another. Generally, however, in Colorado like elevations result in plant populations of quite similar makeup, even though a whole range of mountains or a deep wide valley may lie between. The principal factor causing exceptions to this rule is the tendency of many areas in western Colorado, particularly those between about 6,000 and 10,000 feet in elevation, to receive greater average annual precipitation than is received by corresponding areas east of the Continental Divide. As a result of this, many species which in eastern Colorado occur only in moderately high elevations will be found clear down in the foothills in western sections.

The individual life zones of Colorado are illustrated and described on the next five pages.

UPPER SONORAN ZONE

All of Colorado lying east of the base of the mountains, as well as large areas in western Colorado lying along the course of the Colorado River and its main tributaries, are within the life zone commonly known as the Plains, and referred to in technical books as Upper Sonoran. These areas are mainly below 5500 feet in elevation, and are relatively flat. Clay soils are the rule, with local sandy spots. The rainfall throughout this zone is scanty and irrigation essential to general farming. These conditions have restricted the native vegetation throughout this zone to species which can tolerate long periods of drought, and thrive on sunshine with heat in summer and cold in winter. A surprising number of species of flowering plants live and thrive on these very conditions. We rarely find them in colorful masses, single plants or small colonies being the rule.

Originally native grasses covered this zone with a fairly tight sod, broken, however, by windblown patches and cut by arroyos. Live streams were far apart. Trees were absent except for cottonwoods and a few box elders along water courses. Settlement has brought roads, ditches, cultivated fields and a large amount of livestock. These acts of man have made life hard for some native flowers, but for most species, living opportunity has been increased. The plains are flowerless only for those who fail to pause and search.

The detailed growth patterns or specialized mechanisms by which the various plains flowers resist drought, and so get a chance to live, are numerous. In general they do one or more of these things: rush through a short individual life cycle from seed to seed so timed that the new seed crop is set before the heat of summer is far advanced; conserve the limited moisture their roots gather by having few leaves and defending them from animals by thorns or toughness; or, spend a large part of every year, especially the dry, hot months, as a dormant bulb or buried root stock.

The photograph at top of the page shows a plains area grown with flowering yucca, looking west from the Phipps Highland Ranch just south of Denver.

TRANSITION ZONE

Long strips of land from 5500 to 8000 feet in elevation lying between the plains and the mountains, and filling in with rough hills and valleys the spaces between mountain ranges, comprise a life zone known as the Foothills, and named, by naturalists, the Transition zone. In this zone much of the soil is filled with gravel and weathered rock detritus washed down from higher land or left there by ancient glaciers. Total annual rainfall in this zone is higher than on the plains, and the broken character of the land gives protection from storms.

A greater number of species of flowering plants can be found in this zone than in any other single zone. Local conditions of soil, water and sun exposure vary widely, and these variations offer favorable living conditions to different types of flowering plants and to the numerous shrubs that grow here. Many species of wild flowers which grow on the plains extend into the lower parts of this zone, while other species found in the higher mountains reach down into it, especially along streams.

The chief native trees of this zone are yellow pine and, along streams, narrow leaf cottonwood. Scrub oak covers many hillsides with dense growth, junipers are locally plentiful, and aspens reach down from higher elevations. This tree population attains forest proportions only here and there so that open places for wild flowers are abundant.

In Colorado, visible spring comes earlier in this zone than on the plains below. Sheltered slopes facing the sun pick up the earliest flush of spring green, and by the end of March the very first flowers may here be found in bloom. Late April, May and early June bring the main flower crop. Mass color effects may then be found such as several acres blue with Larkspur, or a whole hillside dotted with red clumps of Lambert's Loco. The main show is over by mid-July, though asters and sunflower-like composites keep the roadsides colorful till frost.

The photograph at the top of the page shows typical scrub oak and ponderosa pine country of the foothills area.

CANADIAN ZONE

The great mid-sections of our high mountains, lying between 8,000 and 10,000 feet in elevation, make up a life zone called Montane, also known as Canadian. Since most of our Colorado mountains are granite, the typical soils in this zone are granite gravel. Some mountains, however, are faulted blocks of sedimentary rock which have weathered into clay and sand soils. The annual rainfall in this zone is over double that of our plains. This has resulted in forests of lodgepole pine, aspens, and of several species of spruce, with stream banks lined with willows and water birch.

This abundance of vegetation has produced enough humus to build rich black soil in the bottoms of the narrow valleys. In this zone grow a wealth of flowering plants. The principal adverse conditions against which they struggle for existence are: a fairly short season from spring melt to fall freeze; and more tree shade and more competition from tree and shrub roots than they would choose. The steep hillsides in this zone may be quite rock covered. Between the rocks small amounts of good soil may form, and under loose rocks moisture stays for a long time. Trees thrive on these hillsides, but in open spots and beside rocky outcrops flowers get their chance. The columbine grows in perfection in this zone, extending downward into the foothills and upward to timberline.

The building of highways in our mountain areas has introduced new conditions of which some plants are quick to take advantage. The stirred-up soil of new road fills and drainage channel construction will be colorful with fireweed, purple fringe, brown-eyed-susans, with here and there penstemons and asters by the second or third season of their use. Local irrigation accomplished by highway drainage and the use of snowplows, as well as distribution of seeds by animals and even by cars that use the roads, all play their part in this quick restoration of life in the soil that has been torn up.

The photograph at top of page shows Echo Lake at an elevation of approximately 10,500 feet. The typical trees are Engelmann spruce, and numerous mountain flowers grow in the moist areas of the foreground.

HUDSONIAN ZONE

Above 10,000 feet the pattern of life changes. Until timberline is reached at about 11,500 feet, this band of mountain country is called the Sub-Alpine or Hudsonian life zone. Soil and moisture conditions are almost as favorable as in the lower montane zone, but here the snows of winter stay late, especially on north slopes, and frost may come even in mid-summer. The race to ripen seed, before winter comes, is intense, and the seeds, when produced and scattered, face special problems of germination and survival.

The trees of this zone are largely Engelmann spruce, limber pine and alpine fir. Some thick forest stands exist, but the main pattern is small compact tree groups—one or more big seed-trees surrounded by younger offspring—with open patches of grass between. Perennial flowering plants, springing from woody root-crowns have special advantages here, though some annuals thrive, especially if they can get started in the fall and remain dormant under snow till spring. Melting snows in May, June and early July give natural irrigation to large areas of this zone. Competition with sedges and grasses and ability to stand light frost are problems for the plants that live here. Many typical alpine plants of the next higher zone work down into these sub-alpine meadows.

The photograph at the top of the page, taken above Echo Lake on the Mt. Evans highway, shows fingers of Engelmann spruce projecting into the treeless tundra area of the Arctic-Alpine.

ARCTIC-ALPINE ZONE

From timberline (about 11,500 feet) up to our highest Colorado mountain summit (Mt. Elbert 14,431 feet) climate is too severe for any trees. This condition marks these areas off as a separate life zone called Alpine or Arctic. Soil forms only slowly on these rocky summits, but mosses, lichens, sedges and grasses have been here for ages of time, all of them patiently building humus. Erosion carries less soil away from the tops than it does from the lower hillsides. So in the spaces between the barren looking rocks, good soil exists, and water, though mainly falling as snow, and not quite as heavily as in the sub-alpine zone below, is adequate for plants. Here grasses, sedges, a few dwarf shrubs and herbaceous plants have all the sunlight to themselves without tree competition. The ever-present adverse condition is low temperature, frequently with strong wind.

It is a land of tough dwarf things. Perennials are the rule, though annuals are found. Low woody mats with basal leaves and flowers only a few inches high are a common pattern. Bulbs and tubers wedge themselves between rocks, out of reach of ground squirrels, if possible. When spring comes with a rush, usually late in June, these dormant plants burst into life in the days of longest sunshine. Shoots of new growth erupt from the ground with buds all formed ready to open. By the end of July the seed crop is largely mature, and by mid-August the browns and crimsons of fall colors in leaves and grasses spread a Persian carpet over these heights. Warm days from then till winter are days of germination for newly scattered seeds and, for established plants, preparation of buds for next year.

It is in this zone of harsh living conditions that some individual plants probably attain greater age than is normally reached by plants of the lower life zones. We know of no statistical study to support this statement, but observation of mats of moss campion, or of tufts of alpine spring beauty, or of scarred old crowns of alpine forget-me-not, indicates that they have safely survived the snow cover of a great many alpine winters.

The view above shows the flower-strewn tundra adjacent to Summit Lake on Mt. Evans at an altitude of over 12,000 feet. In the foreground are masses of alpine avens.

LILY FAMILY

SAND LILY, *Leucocrinum montanum,* NUTT.

Flower is an inch in diameter, of 6 petals and sepals all alike (perianth segments) united at their base into a tube· over an inch long. Several of these rise from the buried crown of the plant, as do also the leaves, ⅜ inch wide and over 6 inches long, resembling heavy curved blades of grass. The matted, cordlike roots store, through the long dormant period, the starches and sugars needed for rapid spring growth. Grows in sandy soil in plains or low foothills. Blooms April-May.

When sand lilies begin to dot the gray plains with their singularly pure white stars we can know that the season of growth and color is returning. We called them Mayflowers and hoped they would be in bloom for May-baskets. They usually were—along with Johnny-jump-ups (little yellow violets) and sprays of pepper an' salt parsley. To pluck them one by one and suck the drop of nectar from the long white tube is one of the delights of childhood. The plants are crowded with flowers during the blooming season, but, when it is over, disappear completely from the scene.

LILY FAMILY

WOOD LILY, *Lilium umbellatum,* PURSH

The flower, of flaring trumpet shape 3 inches in diameter, is formed of 6 petals and sepals, all alike, (perianth segments) tapering at both ends. Color varies from rose-red to red-orange. Stem 15 to 30 inches high, bearing a single flower (occasionally 2 or more) and several whorls of leaves, comes from a round bulb. Picking the flower usually kills the bulb. Grows in rich soil in partial shade near streams, montane zone. Blooms July.

This is one of the most sought-after and breathtaking of our mountain flowers. It used to grow in abundance, then almost disappeared due to excessive picking. Now it is returning in secluded sylvan places. It prefers moist, shady banks where its brilliant color lights the shadows like a flame. The young flowers, with their big dark anthers, are the brightest. As they fade, the anthers shrink and turn dull orange and the flower has a tendency to become spotty. If you have the good luck to find these lilies, stop and enjoy them in their woodsy background—but do not pick any to take home.

LILY FAMILY

MARIPOSA, *Calochortus gunnisonii,* WATS.

Flower, more than 1 inch in diameter, is formed of 3 perianth segments, which are narrow, greenish and sepal-like, and 3 segments which are broad, showy and petal-like. On the inner surface of these latter, near the base, are large, hairy glands of dark color. Stem is slender, 8 to 20 inches tall, with few linear leaves, and comes from a deeply buried corm. Grows in fairly heavy clay soils on open grassy slopes in foothills and lower montane zones. Blooms June-July.

The name mariposa recalls to us the high flat tableland of Mesa Verde with thousands of these delicate lilies floating above the other flowers like butterflies, as the Spanish name implies. Our species is one of the most beautiful, with its tall stem and subtle coloring resembling a small white tulip with grass-like leaves. Other species are creamy, yellow, orange, pink, lavender, gray; some of them quite small, with pointed hairy petals. Journeys to many interesting places will go with a search for the mariposa in its infinite variety of color, shape and habitat.

LILY FAMILY

GLACIER LILY, *Erythronium grandiflorum,* PURSH

    Flowers, 1½ inches across of 6 bright gold perianth segments, all alike and strongly re-curved, nod, singly or in twos or even threes, at the top of a naked scape which rises from the deep-seated bulb. The 6 stamens, each tipped with a large yellow anther, surround a prominent green style and hang downward. Plant is about 10 inches high, with only two broad green leaves which sheath the base of the scape. Grows in sub-alpine zone extending through montane zone. Occurs only on the west side of the Continental Divide (except for a few limited areas immediately on the east side). Blooms immediately after snow melts, which is June in high places.

    Below the snowbanks on Mt. Audubon, near Thunder Lake in Rocky Mountain National Park, on slopes near Rabbit Ears Pass, and in many places on the western side of the range, early summer brings one of the finest flower shows in the west, which it is no exaggeration to call the "field of the cloth of gold." The glacier lily (also called avalanche or snow lily—or, oddly enough—the dogtooth violet) begins to bloom right at the foot of snow banks and follows the retreating ice up the mountainsides. We have seen acres where it was hard to walk without stepping on several plants, particularly in the northern mountains of Wyoming and Montana.

Orchid Family
Yellow Lady's Slipper, *Cypripedium calceolus*, L.

Flower, usually solitary, is shaped like a Dutch shoe about 2 inches long. The sac-like toe part, formed by one of the 3 petals, is bright yellow with greenish sheen, the other 2 petals, much narrower, extend to the sides and are often twisted and streaked with brown. Plant is about 10 inches tall, with broad lance-shaped green leaves which enclose the lower part of the flower stem. Grows on moist but not wet slopes in montane zone. June.

In not too open aspen glades in middle elevations, a privileged seeker after beauty may find this yellow lady's slipper, largest of our native orchids. It is one of several species of *Cypripedium* (the name meaning shoe of Venus) and is sometimes called moccasin flower. A smaller, daintier orchid, the pink *Calypso bulbosa,* is more widely known. This latter likes half sunny edges of our lodgepole forests, being quite dependent on the humic acid of the needles. Often in large groups along the remnants of a decayed tree trunk, they make an entrancing sight, resembling fairy dancers. These are but two of about a dozen orchids that grow wild in Colorado.

Four o'Clock Family

Prairie Snowball, *Abronia fragrans,* NUTT.

Individual flowers are formed of a slender calyx tube, 1 inch long, flaring at its mouth into 5 white, petal-like lobes to make a tiny salver ¼ inch across. They have no true petals. Numerous such flowers are clustered to form the surface of a ball about 2 inches in diameter. Plant has reddish stems, somewhat hairy, that creep on the ground, with fleshy (succulent) green leaves arranged in opposite pairs. Grows in plains on sandy soil. Blooms May-June.

Every plains child knows the prairie snowball—inhabitant of vacant lots in towns, and of dry wind blown flats "in the country." The cluster of starry flowers is indeed round as a snowball and as white—the dark green leaves are in sharp contrast with the bright red stems. The fragrance, almost cloying it is so sweet, perfumes the air of early summer, especially as evening coolness comes. The reddish-purple sand verbena of the southwestern deserts and coastal sand dunes, *Abronia villosa,* is also of this genus. The resemblances are quite apparent.

BUCKWHEAT FAMILY

SULPHUR FLOWER, *Eriogonum umbellatum,* TORR.

Numerous flowers, each formed of 6 minute yellow perianth segments, are grouped in round tight clusters at the ends of slender pedicels, several such clusters radiating to form a flat-topped head (umbel) 4 inches across. These heads are borne on erect hairy leafless stems (scapes) 8 to 15 inches tall. Oblong leaves about $1\frac{1}{2}$ inches long, form a green mat on the ground. Grows on open dry slopes of foothills and lower mountains. Blooms June-September.

Many species of *Eriogonum* are found in Colorado, some of them resembling the one pictured, and some with very different growth habits. This common sulphur flower is one of the finest. Even in bud it is brilliant, for the gold of its flowers, often touched with red, shows before it is quite open. The soft sulphur yellow of the mature flowers gradually changes to shades of orange, maroon and brown as they dry rather than fade. They linger on their stems indefinitely and are fine to mix with grasses and seed pods for a fall bouquet—they might even trim an autumn hat!

Buckwheat Family

Sand Begonia, *Rumex venosus,* PURSH

Flower parts are minute except the three inner sepals which rapidly develop into conspicuous red to rose-colored wings or vanes about $\frac{1}{2}$ inch wide, attached to the seed. These vanes, with their seeds, develop into compact clusters 2 inches or more in diameter. Leaves are oval or oblong, fleshy and dark green, on short stout branches which are often prostrate. Grows in plains. Blooms May-July.

This is just an ordinary dock closely related to the pest you dig from your lawn, but a good example of a common wayside weed brightening the bit of world in which it grows. That bit of world, for this particular dock, is usually an ugly one, as it seems to choose the poorest soil it can find, the cinders beside a railroad track—or the gravelly edge of a country road. No one notices the small, insignificant flower, but its hour of glory comes with the brilliant rose and red seed vanes that call out gaily to every passerby. In the plains of western Colorado another dock, *Rumex hymeno-sepalus,* is also spectacular growing to a height of 2 feet or more with a great column of rose-colored seed vanes.

Purslane Family

Spring Beauty, *Claytonia lanceolata,* PURSH

Flower is ½ inch across of 5 pale rose-colored petals, notched at the end and with veins of darker shade. Sepals are only 2; plant is 6 inches or less in height, with succulent stems and rather broad lance-shaped leaves which rise almost as high as the loose raceme of 3 or more flowers. Grows in rich soil montane and foothill zones. Blooms immediately after snow melts which is late May to July, or much earlier on warm slopes.

The plants of this species that grow in foothill locations often have quite bright rosy color. They are great favorites, as their first blooms hint that winter is nearly over and spring on the way. They have been reported as early as January, and by mid-March they are often abundant under scrub oaks on sunny foothill slopes. The east side of the Hogsback near Golden is a good place to find early ones. The plant pictured above has the pale color and general growth habit of those that grow high in the montane zone. It often forms a carpet or ground cover of pale pink bloom in the fields of glacier lilies. Another species, *Claytonia megarhiza,* has a big root, to store food and moisture, and grows in the alpine zone. We have found plants of it on the big flat summit of Pikes Peak where other signs of spring are few.

Pink Family

Moss Campion, *Silene acaulis,* L.

Flowers, ⅜ inch across, of 5 bright purplish-red petals, notched at the end, spread from the top of a tubular calyx so that the whole flower forms a tiny salver. Stems and leaves are so dwarfed and tightly grouped as to give the appearance of a cushion of green moss 3 to 8 inches across, studded with little reddish stars. Grows in alpine rocky areas extending to peak summits. Blooms late June-early July.

This is one of the alpine flowers we share with all the alpine and arctic lands of the Northern Hemisphere. High mountain ridges are its home here, and if we travel north we keep finding it at progressively lower elevations until it reaches the low barren lands of the arctic. Always it is where winds are cold and climate is too rough for trees. You might take it for a pad of green moss if it were not for its red flowers, often in the form of a circlet near the plant's edge. Close examination shows a full-fledged plant, however, with leaves, stems and a stout tap-root well buried in what soil there is below and around the rock it presses against. Another member of the pink family that grows as a mat against our timberline rocks is sandwort, *Arenaria sajanensis.* Its flowers are white, and the plant less densely compacted. Related to both of these alpine pinks are the numerous chickweeds of foothills and mountains. They have low slender stems and their petals are white and deeply notched at the end.

BUTTERCUP FAMILY

PASQUE FLOWER, *Pulsatilla ludoviciana,* HELLER

Flowers, of 5 to 7 petal-like sepals, form a wide cup 1½ inches across, white or pale lavender within, and much darker lavender to purple, covered with silky hairs, on the outside. The numerous golden stamens are prominent. The flower buds, quite furry at this stage, spring directly from a buried root crown before the green leaves, divided into several lobes, appear. Grows in foothills, especially on gentle north slopes where extra snow has drifted. Blooms late March-April.

It goes also by the name of wind-flower, and often is called anemone. Whatever name you choose, it is one of the best-loved flowers of the Rockies. They are with us in March, going on into April, coming up through late snows—keeping themselves warm with their furs about them. The flowers start on short stems, but the whole plant grows quite large and "leggy" as the season advances, and finally the fluffy seed plumes offer their wares to every breeze. This same pasque flower is the state flower of South Dakota. A northern species, growing in Glacier Park and in Canada, *Pulsatilla occidentalis,* has larger flowers, of a creamy color. Its cluster of seed plumes is large and dense enough to resemble a dish mop.

Buttercup Family

Globe Anemone, *Anemone globosa,* NUTT.

Flower, ¾ inch in diameter, of 5 to 9 showy petal-like sepals, usually deep red, occasionally yellow, forms a shallow cup around the numerous stamens and a conspicuous group of pistils which, after the flower fades, become a round thimble-shaped seed cluster. The pedicels, bearing the solitary flowers at their tips, are several inches long and covered with silky hairs. Plant is about 1 foot tall, with subdivided leaves near the base and on the sparingly branched stems. Grows in partial shade in montane zone. Blooms June-July.

This globe anemone, related to the better known pasque flower, is one of the many less conspicuous plants that add to the charm of a flowery hillside, yet reserve their more delicate beauty for those who take time to prowl. This particular specimen was found in a glade filled with columbines. We would probably not have seen it if we had not stopped to try one more columbine picture! *Anemone canadensis* is a somewhat larger plant with pure white flowers, rather woody stems and deep green foliage. It grows in shady places along foothill streams, but only where conditions are to its liking. In these spots it forms rather dense colonies.

BUTTERCUP FAMILY
NELSON'S LARKSPUR, *Delphinium nelsonii,* GREENE

Flowers, ½ inch or more wide, are formed of 5 showy, dark blue, irregularly shaped sepals, enclosing at their base 4 much smaller petals of lighter color. The uppermost sepal extends backward as a slender spur ½ inch or more in length. About a dozen flowers on slender pedicels group around a central erect stem to form a loose raceme which often nods slightly at the top. Plant is 10 to 15 inches tall and bears rather few leaves each sub-divided into linear segments. Grows in foothills zone. Blooms late April to early June.

This small larkspur of the early spring looks much like the single larkspur of an old-fashioned garden. Its favorite location is near the base of a clump of scrub oak where a little snow has drifted in the winter giving that spot a bit of extra water. The intense blue of these flowers contrasts well with the leather brown color of last season's oak leaves. When spring is farther advanced other taller larkspurs, such as *Delphinium geyeri,* called poison-weed by the stockmen, make a more spectacular showing on low foothills and plains. All of the larkspurs contain an alkaloid poison which is deadly to cattle and somewhat dangerous to other stock.

Buttercup Family
Snow Buttercup, *Ranunculus adoneus,* Gray

Flowers are an inch across, formed of several (3 to 15) broad, over-lapping golden petals having the glossy sheen of butter. The sparse leaves are divided into linear lobes. These and the succulent stems grow a few inches tall, breaking out of frosty soil with flower bud ready to open. Grows on alpine and sub-alpine slopes near snow banks. Blooms when snow melts, usually June to early July.

The hardiness of the snow buttercup is its outstanding characteristic. It comes up through the snow because in the high altitude in which it lives its time for fruition is short. It pushes a stout knuckle of stem through the snow crust, attracting the sun's heat by the dark color of its stem, then the knuckle straightens, lifting the already formed bud into an erect position. The bud opens rapidly and proceeds to spread out in the hole caused by melting. Of the many glossy members of the buttercup family, there are few of so rich a yellow, or which give such an appearance of being all flower with inconsiderable leaf and stem.

BUTTERCUP FAMILY

GLOBEFLOWER, *Trollius laxus,* SALISB.

Flower is 1¼ inches across of 5 to 10 (or more) pale cream petal-like sepals, with numerous yellow stamens and several pistils in the center. Numerous petals, so dwarfed as hardly to be noticed, surround the base of the stamens. Plants, 8 to 15 inches tall, often grow in groups and bear several flowers, each on its own slender stem. Leaves are dark green and deeply cut into 5 or more spreading lobes (palmate). Grows in moist rich soil in sub-alpine and alpine zones. Blooms late May-July.

When the snowbanks melt in the alpine country, hundreds of temporary runlets carry the snow water to timberline lakes and to permanent streams. In the wet soil along these runlets and near these lakes, globe-flower is one of the common and very good looking plants. Both its foliage and its flowers are graceful and charming. Associated with it is usually marsh marigold, *Caltha rotundifolia,* which is also a member of the buttercup family. Our Colorado marsh marigold is not gold at all, but white—even a bluish-white. It grows with its feet right in the water. Its leaves are entire and are all at the base of the sturdy low plant. Its flowers are as large or slightly larger than those of globeflower. It makes an effective companion for its more dainty relative.

Buttercup Family

Columbine, *Aquilegia coerulea,* JAMES

The flower is formed of 5 sepals and 5 petals, alternately arranged and all of them showy. The sepals are deep blue or sometimes quite pale, forming a wide saucer-like star 3 inches across; the petals form a white inner cup 1¾ inches across, and stretch back between the sepals as hollow, slender 2-inch spurs. Plants are 2 feet or more high of several delicate stems, usually carrying at their tops numerous flowers. The deeply cut leaves are mainly concentrated at the plant base. Grows in rich soil in montane zone, but extends into foothills and up to timberline. Blooms June-July.

Colorado's queenly state flower speaks for itself much more eloquently than humans can speak for it. No portrait can do it justice. We have found it in the very glade near Palmer Lake where James first saw it and named it *coerulea* for its celestial blue. We have found it in countless aspen groves of the montane zone and finally on rocky scree near timberline (a more compact plant there—with flowers sometimes white or of a rosy hue). Always there is the thrill of real discovery—a new realization of its beauty. A less common and even more exciting find is the dwarf columbine, *Aquilegia saximontana,* that grows between rocks above timberline.

Poppy Family

Prickly Poppy, *Argemone intermedia,* sweet

Flower, 3 inches or more across, is formed of 6 brilliant white, paper-like petals, surrounding numerous golden stamens with, at the very center, a dark or even black stigma. Blossoms, in loose clusters opening over a long period, crowd each other slightly at the tops of the branching stems. Plant is 2 to 5 feet tall, with gray-green leaves divided into lobes, and with yellowish spines along the stems and leaf ribs. Grows in plains, foothills and lower montane zones. Blooms May-September.

These big coarse plants, which may be seen in small groups along our roads at culvert ends and in neglected fence rows, could be taken for some sort of thistle if it were not for the amazing flowers which they display in successive crops throughout the whole summer. The blossoms look like big circles of white crepe paper with a center of spun gold. As the season advances, the plants get ragged, but even in September a few fresh flowers will appear. Some resemblance can be seen between these blossoms and the Oriental poppies of our gardens, but only by study of their botanical structure can we find why they are put in the same family with golden smoke, *Corydalis aurea,* of our foothills, and the bleeding-heart of old-fashioned gardens.

MUSTARD FAMILY

WALLFLOWER, *Erysimum asperum,* DC.

Flowers, 1/2 inch in diameter, are formed of 4 petals arranged like a Maltese cross, yellow to orange in color. They are clustered into a round terminal head, the lower flowers of which open first so that usually tubular seed pods (siliques) have formed near the base by the time the top of the cluster is in bloom. Plants are 8 inches or more high, of several stems from one root crown. Grows in foothills, extending down to plains and up through montane zone. Blooms May-July.

The mustards are legion. Fields of them add a yellow note to many western hillsides. They range from weedy poor relations, like shepherd's purse, to tall, showy spikes of prince's plume, *Stanleya apinnata.* Wall-flower—despite its name suggesting a colorless personality—is one of the handsome children of the family. Its flowers, larger than most mustards, range in color from pale yellow, through orange, to rich bronze shades. By no means all of the mustards are yellow. The flowers of many of them are white, some, like the cardamine that grows in abundance along sub-alpine water runs, being a very showy, brilliant white.

Saxifrage Family

Snowball Saxifrage, *Saxifraga rhomboidea*, GREENE

Individual flowers are ¼ inch or less across, each with 5 white petals, and are grouped in a compact, round-topped head about 1 inch in diameter which forms the top of a naked stem (scape). This scape rises to a height of 8 inches, or sometimes much less, from the center of a flat circle of oblong, leathery leaves. As the blossoms age, the flower cluster becomes loose and sprangly. Grows on moist slopes in sub-alpine and montane zones. Blooms May-July.

Saxifrage is another large family of quite varied sorts. Gooseberries and mock orange come within its membership. The numerous species of alum root, *Heuchera*, are also included, as are many little alpine and sub-alpine plants that grow out of rock crevices in our high mountains. Purple saxifrage, *Saxifraga jamesii*, with quite large red-purple flowers, and dotted saxifrage, *Saxifraga austromontana*, with tiny white flowers covered with pale dots, are among the best. All of these seem able to thrive on only a teaspoonful of soil in a rock crack, if only there is local moisture. The structural features that bring all these plants within one family are not obvious. The leaves of many of them are similar to the leaves of a gooseberry bush, though in some this resemblance is remote, and in others entirely absent.

ORPINE FAMILY

QUEEN'S CROWN, *Sedum rhodanthum,* GRAY

Individual flowers, ¼ inch across, are formed of 4 or 5 bright rose petals; numerous flowers being congested in a round head an inch or more in diameter terminating a leafy shoot, several of which rise from a woody root crown. Plant is 6 to 10 inches high, with narrow, gray-green, fleshy leaves crowded along the succulent stems. Grows in wet places alpine and sub-alpine zones. Blooms June-August.

Along the cold, mountain stream trickling out from Lake Isabelle, or near any similar alpine lake or tarn, grows the *Sedum,* named queen's crown for the rosy-pink crowns of blossoms. These plants like to have their feet in the water and often help to make the hillocky mounds on the lake's edge. Nearby and tolerating drier ground, is the king's crown, *Sedum integri-folium,* with its flatter head of deep maroon flowers resembling the old-fashioned Bohemiam garnet jewelry. The stems and leaves of these sedums color brilliantly with the first frosts and add richness to the Persian carpets of timberline in late August and early September.

Rose Family

Bush Cinquefoil, *Potentilla fruticosa,* L.

Flowers are an inch in diameter, of 5 broad, golden petals surrounding 20 or more stamens. Groups of several flowers are borne at the ends of the numerous short branches. Plant is a dense shrub about 3 to 4 feet high with many dark, woody, freely-branching stems. Leaves are pinnate, with usually 5 or 7 narrow linear leaflets. Grows in moist parts of the montane zone, also in the upper foothills and the lower sub-alpine zones. Blooms continuously May to September.

This thornless yellow rose is one of the most widespread and most ornamental shrubs of mountain areas. Individual clumps are rarely fully covered with bloom at any one time, tending rather to bring out a few fresh flowers each day of the season so that all summer long there are buds, fresh blossoms, groups of faded petals, and small, dry, fuzzy seeds (achenes) distributed over the plant. Other species of *Potentilla* grow also in our mountains. They are much smaller and most of them herb-like, but the resemblance to a yellow single rose, and the absence of thorns are common to them all. We have many wild roses in this same family, of the genus *Rosa,* that have plenty of thorns and closely resemble the red single roses of the garden.

Pea Family

Prairie Pea, *Lathyrus stipulaceus,* B. AND ST. J.

Flowers, more than ½ inch across, are shaped like a cultivated sweet pea, with very showy red banner and paler lateral petals and keel. Plants, about 6 inches high, grow in irregular mats. The leaves are pinnate, formed by about 4 pairs of narrow linear leaflets. These and the stems are gray-green and, in most plains specimens, covered with rather silky down. Grows in sandy soil on plains. Blooms May-June.

This, and the quite different looking plants shown on the next three pages, give but a small sample of the pea family, which is one of the largest and most important of the plant groups. More than 150 species in this one family are native to Colorado, and additional ones have been introduced for ornament or food. They take every form and size from the little flat mats of deer clover, shown on the opposite page, to the rank growing clumps of sweet clover that spread themselves along our roads. Beans and alfalfa as well as sweet peas, lupines and even locust trees, all belong to this big family.

PEA FAMILY

DEER CLOVER, *Trifolium nanum,* TORR.

Individual flowers, pink-lavender to purple, formed along a keel, like those of the cultivated clovers, about $\frac{1}{2}$ inch long and rather slender, grow singly or in twos or threes on short pedicels rising directly from the root crown. The plant is a dense mat, often a foot or more across, covered with small 3-foliate leaves. Grows on rocky flats or slopes in alpine zone. Blooms June-July.

For many, acquainted only with the cultivated clovers of lawn and meadow, it is a pleasure to know that the high pastures grazed by deer and elk have clovers as well. At least three species are familiar to observing travelers along Trail Ridge, or up Mt. Evans, or along any road that crosses the enchanted land where trees stop and dwarfed plant life takes over. The deer clover pictured here likes rocky places. Its flowers are packed close together, but not clustered in heads as are those of its alpine neighbor, *Trifolium dasyphyllum,* which closely resembles the white clover of our lawns, though with touches on its petals of red-brown. In the high places, extending down through the sub-alpine zone there is also a bright red clover, *Trifolium parryi,* smaller but otherwise much like the cultivated red clover.

Pea Family

Lambert's Loco, *Oxytropis lambertii,* PURSH

Individual flowers, about $\frac{1}{2}$ inch wide, are formed of 5 dissimilar petals, usually magenta red, sometimes other shades from rose to purple. The banner bends back slightly and carries markings of lighter color near its base; the 2 lateral petals are plain and angle forward; the 2 lower petals form a narrow keel. Numerous flowers, attached at the calyx base along the upper third of a naked stem, form a showy spike 10 inches or more tall, several of which rise from one root crown. Leaves, pinnate, with numerous green leaflets, rise also from the root crown and are about half the height of the flower spikes. Grows in foothills and higher parts of plains zone. Blooms May-July.

The many members of the pea family going by the names of loco, vetch, milk vetch, etc., are usually considered crass weeds and are in disrepute because some of them are poisonous to stock. They often grow in soil containing traces of selenium, and are doubly harmful in that case. Where other browze is good, animals usually leave the toxic ones alone, except the occasional horse that becomes "an addict" and is "locoed." In spite of these obnoxious qualities, there are few plants that give more bright and decorative touches to the plains.

Pea Family

Golden Banner, *Thermopsis divaricarpa,* A. NELS.

The individual flowers are about ¾ inch across, each formed of 5 dissimilar golden petals. The top petal is an upright banner, with a wing petal on each side and in the center the 2 keel petals folded together. A dozen or more flowers are attached by short pedicels to the upper part of the stem, forming a loose raceme. Plants, of one or several erect leafy stems from a root crown, are 1-2 feet tall. Grows in foothills and montane zones. Blooms April-July.

Several closely allied species share the name of golden banner, and among them cover a very wide range in all parts of Colorado from the plains well into the mountains. They spread both by seeds and by root-runners resulting in quite large colonies. They seem to be unpalatable to livestock so, in spite of their attractive looking leaves, they stay fresh while other plants around them look browzed. Everywhere they are gay and decorative. A bright field of them near the Platte River, bowing to the wind, banks of them in open glades of the Greenhorn Mountains, and pale yellow clumps along the trail to Lulu City, are prized flower memories.

Loasa Family

Stickweed, *Mentzelia nuda,* T. AND G.

Flowers, about 2 inches wide, are formed of 10 narrow, creamy, petals which spread wide and surround a radiating cluster of 100 or more pale stamens as long as the petals. Plant is 2 to 4 feet high of white shiny stems branching freely from one main stem, and rather sparsely covered with deeply indented, light green leaves of a peculiar rough texture. Grows on plains and low foothills. Blooms July-August.

The leaves of this plant are covered with minute barbed hairs which cling to cloth so firmly that a spray of several flowers placed upon a coat lapel will stay almost as dependably as if fastened with a pin. They have the feel of fine-grained sandpaper. The flowers are very responsive to light conditions. All through the morning and well into the afternoon they are tightly closed, then about four o'clock, or a half hour earlier if clouds reduce the light, they spread into full bloom. This opening proceeds so rapidly that the movement of the petals is quite easily seen. In a period of twenty minutes or less a colony of the plants will change its whole appearance from inconspicuous weeds to a gorgeous display of big pale stars. A related species, *Mentzelia decapetala,* has even larger flowers of deeper cream color. It waits until after sundown to open.

Cactus Family

Strawberry Cactus, *Echinocereus triglochidiatus,* ENGELM.

Flowers are brilliant scarlet, $2\frac{1}{2}$ inches across, with a conspicuous group of green stigmas in the center. Plant is a single, erect, cylindrical, dark-green joint or stem about 5 inches high, several to many of which often group closely together forming a mound. The stems are strongly ridged and carry sharp spines in clusters. Grows in rocky or gravelly soil on plains and into foothills, southwestern Colorado. Blooms May.

This is related to some larger *cacti* that grow in Arizona, and there get the name of hedgehog. The name pincushion is broadly used for all the small round *cacti* of our area even though they are not too closely related to each other. The bright, strawberry-red flowers of the plant shown above quite set it apart from the pincushions of eastern Colorado plains. Among these are hen-and-chickens cactus, *Echinocereus vividiflorus,* with small, greenish-yellow flowers, also, spiny stars, *Coryphantha vivipara,* a round little cactus with shiny purple flowers. These plants are so like the prairie sod in color as to defy search when not in bloom. Ball cactus, *Pediocactus simpsonii,* of foothills and montane zones, is quite a perfect globe in shape, 3 to 6 inches in diameter, and has small pink flowers closely grouped at the top of the globe.

Cactus Family

Grizzly Bear Cactus, *Opuntia trichophora,* BRITTON AND ROSE

Flowers are 3 inches or more across, usually light-yellow with fine sheen, several of them erupting from the edge of a flat, oval joint. Plant spreads over a circular area, about 2 feet in diameter, and is made up of numerous connected flat joints, of light-green color, all heavily armored with pale, sharp spines, some of which, in old plants, may be flexible and hair-like. Grows on clay soil in foothills and plains of middle and western Colorado. Blooms June-early July.

Several species of *Opuntia* closely resemble each other. Some of them, including a few found in Colorado, bear soft, juicy fruits which are quite good eating when the prickles on the skins are removed, so all of them are called prickly pear. The one shown above grows freely on the high grassy flats of the San Luis Valley. It bears dry, hard fruits, as do most of our Colorado species. The prickly pears, like all the other *cacti*, accumulate moisture, when they get a chance, in the soft pulp of their round or jointed stems. Then, over periods of drought, this moisture is used to produce flowers, to mature seeds and to keep the plant alive. The whole plant shrinks visibly if the times between drinks are long. But for the defensive armor of their spines, few of them would survive, because in a thirsty land every hungry cow is looking for moisture too.

Evening Primrose Family
Yellow Evening Primrose, *Oenothera brachycarpa,* GRAY

Flowers are cadmium-yellow, fading old-rose, 2½ inches across, of 4 wide petals. The 4 narrow sepals bend back and at their base merge into a hollow tubular stem. The style branches at its tip into 4 conspicuous slender stigmas. Plant has little or no main stem; leaves are dark-green, strap-shaped, 3 inches long. Grows in foothills, but only where soil is somewhat marly. Blooms May-June.

Look for this one of our numerous evening-primroses about Memorial Day. Soil formed from the disintegration of Niobrara shale such as we find along the Hogsback near Denver, or along the Boulder-Lyons road, is its preference. The plants are rather ragged, but the flowers draw all our attention to their soft, clear yellow as they spread open in the sunshine. They last but a day—fading into soft rosy colors. The white members of this family are much better known. Several such species common on the plains are so responsive to early summer rain that within days after a good shower all our roadsides and even vacant lots will be gay with their short-lived beauty.

Evening Primrose Family

Fireweed, *Epilobium angustifolium*, L.

Individual flowers, 1 inch across, are formed of 4 wide-spreading, magenta petals, and are attached by longish pedicels to a central stem, so that the whole flower cluster (inflorescence) is a loose raceme forming the top foot or more of a tall leafy shoot, several of which rise from a woody root crown. Leaves are narrow, 2 inches or more in length. The entire plant is often 4 feet or more tall. Grows in sunny openings in montane zone. Blooms June-August.

Webster's Dictionary describes fireweed as "any of several weeds, troublesome in clearings or burned districts." To use "troublesome" in connection with this great "willow-herb" of the Rockies seems most unkind. We are grateful to have it rush into devastated areas to cover scars with its bright pink to magenta blossoms. The whole plant reddens as it ages. The flower matures into a long thin pod which splits and curls releasing feathery seed carriers. A less common low growing species with larger flowers and broader leaves, *Epilobium latifolium,* also grows in the area. It is a real find. A few grow not far below Loveland Pass.

Heath Family
Pipsissewa, *Chimaphila umbellata*, NUTT.

Flower, ½ inch across, formed of 5 rose-pink petals that bend back and surround, at the center, a conspicuous bright green ovary which is tipped with a disc-like stigma. The 10 prominent stamens, spreading from near the base of the ovary, look like short claws. Plant is 8-12 inches tall, bearing a cluster of several flowers at its top. Leaves are shiny and evergreen with saw-toothed edges, arranged in whorls along the woody stems, but most numerous at the base of the plant. Grows in moist acid soil under pine or spruce trees in montane zone. Blooms late July-August.

The members of the heath family like shade, acid soil and moisture. These conditions they find in the woods of the Northwest, where a great variety of them, including rhododendrons and azaleas, grow in abundance. Colorado has its share of the smaller heaths for those who look for them in shady spots and along mossy trails near mountain streams. The trail to Calypso Falls in Rocky Mountain National Park is good hunting, not only for pipsissewa, but for the pyrolas and for the tiny white wood-nymph, *Moneses uniflora,* all of them heaths. Kinnikinnick, *Arctostaphylos uva-ursi,* is a heath of prostrate growth habit quite common on mountain slopes. Bright red berries remain among its evergreen leaves until Christmas.

Primrose Family

Brook Primrose, *Primula parryi,* GRAY

Individual flowers, almost $\frac{1}{2}$ inch across, are formed of 5 brilliant, crimson, spreading corolla lobes which join at their base into a narrow tube; dark shadings and yellow markings at the throat of the tube give the effect of a round eye. A dozen or more flowers, each on a nodding pedicel, are clustered at the top of a stout dark stem which rises from a whorl of deep-green, broad, lance-shaped leaves. Plant is about 10 to 20 inches tall. Grows in sub-alpine zone or slightly higher. Blooms June-early July.

This spectacular primrose grows at the edge of cold streams, or often on rocky-mossy hillocks right in mid-stream. One never forgets the picture of their beauty—the flower clusters so rich in color, the alpine background, the mat of moss and deep green leaves. Too bad for such a plant to spoil any part of it with a most disagreeable fragrance, yet that does remove any temptation to take them home. On the higher tundras, a charming find is the tiny fairy primrose, *Primula angustifolia,* similar in color, though not so vivid. A single short-stemmed flower is usually all that this plant carries.

PRIMROSE FAMILY

SHOOTING STAR, *Dodecatheon radicatum,* GREENE

Individual flowers, ¾ inch across, are formed of 5 crimson, rather narrow, petals or corolla lobes which flare outward and backward, but unite at their base into a short tube. From this tube 5 conspicuous anthers, over ¼ inch long, grouped together like a sharp straight beak, protrude forward. Ten or more flowers, each on a slender pedicel, nod in a cluster at the top of a stout scape which rises 10 to 15 inches high from a basal mat of dark-green, oblong leaves. Grows along streams and in wet meadows, in montane and sub-alpine zones. Blooms June-early July.

Both the coloring and the shape of this little flower are fancy indeed. It is small wonder that such names as shooting-star and bird-bill have been given it. The crimson of its petals contrasts strongly with its conspicuous almost black "bill," and between these colors is a little circlet of white, often shaded with yellow markings. A whole meadow of such flowers is a sight well worth a trip to South Park, or to other of our high meadow areas, where shooting-stars can be found in profusion. In blooming season they follow the wild iris and, in turn, they are followed by the low, red lousewort, *Pedicularis crenulata,* all of which can in favorable seasons give fine mass color effects.

Gentian Family

Fringed Gentian, *Gentiana elegans,* A. NELS.

Flowers are 2 to 3 inches long, of 4 deep purple-blue petals, fitted together to form a square column for over half their length, then, in sunlight, flaring outward to exhibit fringed tops and upper edges. Each flower is at the end of a stem which bears several pairs of oblong, opposite leaves. Plants are about 12 inches high of several erect stems branching from near the base. Grows in sub-alpine wet meadows. Blooms August-September.

The lush hay meadows of Colorado's upland parks are bright through the summer with a succession of flowers. Late in the season come the gentians. There are several species of these (we have counted a dozen on a single trip), some of them quite uninteresting, weedy plants. The queen of them is the fringed gentian, growing in abundance along the edge of these high hay meadows, and even persisting in the stubble after haying is past. A few of them last into late September. The flowers close up under cloudy skies, but to find masses of them full-open on a sunny day, when they display their fringed petals and large golden stamens, is a heart-warming experience to be treasured for flowerless days ahead.

Milkweed Family

Milkweed, *Asclepias speciosa*, TORR.

Individual flower is a rosy, 5-point, star about ⅜ inch across, at the center of which is a group of 5 small appendages curving inward and forming a crown around the style and stamens. Numerous flowers cluster together into a ball about 3 inches in diameter. Plants are about 3 feet tall with thick broad leaves, the flower clusters borne at the top of the stem and in axils of upper leaves. Grows on plains, especially along ditch banks. Blooms June-July.

The common weeds are too often taken for granted and not appraised for their real beauty. This milkweed is in such a group—a coarse-growing plant along country roads, often dust covered, yet with flowers of fine delicate color and real charm whether we examine them singly or fix our attention on the compact cluster in which they grow. As autumn comes the dry leaves do not drop, but cling to the stem, rattling in the wind. The rough seed pods, often four inches long, turn a rich brown, and finally split open revealing a filling of lustrous, silky, down from which is gradually released the seeds—brown-clad paratroopers with the most airy-fairy parachutes in the world.

Morning-Glory Family
Bush Morning-Glory, *Ipomoea leptophylla,* TORR.

The flowers, shaped like pink trumpets with maroon striations, 3 inches long and 2 inches across the mouth, are scattered freely along the outer third of the stout yellowish stems which form a thick bush 2 feet or more high. New buds coming out each day keep the plant in bloom for the morning hours of several weeks. Leaves are narrow and linear, 2 inches long; the root is large and spongy. Grows in sandy soil on plains. Blooms July.

This morning-glory is no clinging vine, even though its flowers—like those of its cultivated relative on the back yard fence—do open only in the coolness of dawn and wither in the heat of noon. For all the sturdiness of individual plants, with their roots going "clear to China," they do not seem to multiply rapidly and colonies of them may be miles apart. There are some fine bushes on the sandy hills along the Denver-Parker road, but the colony is becoming smaller rather than expanding. The common bindweed, *Convolvulus arvenis,* is a member of this same family. Its ability to spread rapidly along roads and into cultivated fields makes it a serious pest.

Waterleaf Family

Purple Fringe, *Phacelia sericea,* Gray

Numerous purple flowers, each ¼ inch in diameter, crowd at and near the top of an erect hairy stem, making a cylindrical flower spike 3 inches or more in length. The 5 stamens of each flower are tipped with bright golden anthers and stick out farther than the petals, giving the effect of gold-headed pins radiating from a purple cushion. Plant is 6 to 12 inches tall of several leafy stems from a woody crown, the leaves divided into numerous narrow lobes. Grows in rather dry soil, montane to sub-alpine zones. Blooms May-July.

Many other species of *Phacelia* live in desert places where we have learned to know and admire them, but our first acquaintance—and last love—is this purple fringe of the montane zone. Its color is deeper, more velvety, and the pollen of its anthers brighter gold than most of its desert brethren can boast. It keeps, however, considerable tolerance for dry places, so that fresh road-fills are gay with it. The mountaineer who views his flowers only from a car has no excuse for not knowing this one.

Borage Family

Alpine Forget-Me-Not, *Eritrichium elongatum,* johnston

Flowers, ⅜ inch in diameter, are formed of deep-blue (occasionally white) petals, spreading into a little flat disc and joining at their base into a short tube. Minute golden crests in the throat of this corolla tube, often bordered by white, give the effect of a central eye. Plant is formed of a tough woody root crown bearing several very short leafy shoots with flower clusters at the top. Entire plant is compact, covered with short silky hairs, and rarely 3 inches high. Grows on flat spots between rocks in alpine zone extending clear to peak summits. Blooms late June-early July.

The plant "association" pictured above is such as we find on Trail Ridge. It has bright lichen, sedum, polemonium and alpine forget-me-not— the kind of miniature garden that makes high altitude flower hunting so much fun. The woody base of the forget-me-not is built to stand the cold of long winters. The flowers—tiny and delicate for so rugged a habitat— are of heaven's own blue. Their exquisite perfume is elusive. Only once have we found them in such abundance that the fragrance called out to tell us where they were hiding. Their range is wide, however, and in the short blossoming season there is a good chance of finding a few on the slopes of any of our high peaks.

PHLOX FAMILY

SKY PILOT, *Polemonium viscosum,* NUTT.

Numerous violet-blue flowers, each about ½ inch across, of 5 rounded corolla lobes joining in a funnel-like tube, are clustered into a head about 2½ inches in diameter, which nods slightly on its erect stem. Plants are about 8 inches high, with numerous bright-green, pinnate leaves cut into many narrow leaflets. The leaves may be erect or may interweave somewhat at the base of a close group of several plants. Grows in rocky places, alpine zone. Blooms late June-early July.

The sky pilot, growing among rocks up where the sky seems very near, reflects its blue and so is supposed to direct our thoughts upward. This same feeling is embodied in the name of another species of *Polemonium,* Jacobs ladder, *Polemonium pulcherrimum,* the staggered leaves of which may represent the steps by which we climb. Sky pilot seems very much affected by the particular season. In a dry summer, it is straggly and manages to produce only a few blooms of faded blue. In a good year, large clumps of sturdy erect plants make patches of deep color, accented by their golden stamens. The leaves have a strong, offensive odor, but the flowers are honey sweet.

PHLOX FAMILY

SCARLET GILIA, *Gilia aggregata,* SPRENG.

Individual flower, $1\frac{1}{2}$ inches long, is formed of a slender trumpet-like, bright-scarlet (sometimes coral pink) corolla flaring at the mouth into 5 narrow lobes. Numerous flowers attached by short pedicels, are carried in small groups along one side of the green stem. Plant is about 18-24 inches tall, usually of one main stem, with sometimes a few branches. Leaves are deeply cut into thin linear subdivisions, usually curved. Grows in plains and foothills zones. Blooms June-August.

In many otherwise barren areas, the red gilia or sky rocket plant spreads its blaze of color in large patches or hangs, a single wand of bloom, over the edge of the trail. It keeps blooming through the summer, a few stragglers holding on till Labor Day. In early September we have found them in the Wet Mountain Valley brightening the brown of the autumn grasses. A white species, *Gilia attenuata,* tends to grow at lower elevations —the red higher in the foothills. The pale pink and coral plants are probably hybrids.

Figwort Family

Indian Paintbrush, *Castilleja integra*, GRAY

The true flowers are slender, two-lipped tubes of pale or greenish color about 1 inch long. They are surrounded and often completely hidden by the conspicuous, brick-red, modified leaves (bracts) which form a flower-like cluster at the upper ends of the stems. The bract colors in this species vary considerably through several shades of red. Plant is 8-15 inches tall composed of several leafy stems, very tough and woody at their lower ends, rising from a woody root crown. Grows in foothills and higher plains, extending upward through montane zone. Blooms June-July.

In the early summer, this spectacular plant may be seen in the prairie stretches along the highway between Denver and Colorado Springs—or a bit later in the season—literally carpeting the drier areas of South Park. In higher altitudes, particularly in the well-watered vales of Engelmann spruce, there are other species with bracts of brilliant shades of rose and maroon. In those same high gardens and on above timberline there is a yellow paintbrush. The fortunate flower hunter may even be rewarded by a yellow one tipped with red—or red edged with yellow.

FIGWORT FAMILY

PENSTEMON, *Penstemon unilateralis,* RYDB.

Individual flower is about ½ inch wide and somewhat longer, formed of a bell-shaped, lavender-blue corolla which flares at its mouth into 5 lobes separated into two groups. Numerous flowers, in groups of 3 or more, are closely arranged along one side of the top half of each stem, several stems rising from a root crown. Plant is 2 feet or more tall, with narrow tapering leaves, opposite each other in pairs. Grows in foothills and montane zones. Blooms late June-July.

This is but one of twenty or more species of *Penstemon* found in Colorado. Some, such as *Penstemon angustifolius,* with its azure blue flowers, grow on the plains. A few are dwarf species of the sub-alpine zone such as *Penstemon harbourii.* Every zone and every section has its quota, and they range in color through all shades of lavender, blue, purple, and even red. In details of flower structure, as well as in size, they vary considerably. All of them, however, have a tubular corolla of some shape, terminating in five lobes, divided into two groups, giving them a two-lipped appearance. From this their relationship to garden snapdragons is apparent. In the penstemons, also, the topmost of their five stamens is sterile and often tipped with a little brush of hairs. This gives them the name of beardstongue.

COMPOSITE FAMILY

GAILLARDIA, *Gaillardia aristata,* PURSH

Flower head, 3 inches or more across, is formed of a central red disk made up of many minute tubular flowers (florets), surrounded by an outer circle of long flat golden rays cleft at tips into 3 teeth. Plants are 2 feet or more high of several rough stems usually erect, but sometimes contorted. The dark green leaves are lance-shaped and rough. Grows in foothills. Blooms June-July.

Do you have one just like this in your garden? Cultivation has changed the gaillardia less than it has most native plants. It was born a handsome, showy flower. There is charm in its notched rays and in the way the red of the central disk flowers runs outward into the gold of the rays, as though the painter had been careless with his brush and lavish with his colors. It grows far beyond the limits of Colorado. In the rough breaks of the Montana hills several separate plants will spread out and interweave as a colorful mass, giving it there the name "blanket-flower."

COMPOSITE FAMILY

RABBIT BRUSH, *Chrysothamnus nauseosus,* H. AND C.

Individual flower heads are about ¼ inch across and double that in length, each formed of a dozen or more tubular bright gold florets closely compressed at their bases into a green involucre. Numerous such heads are clustered loosely together into round-topped groups (cymes) at the ends of stems and branches. Plant is a wide-branching, woody shrub 2-4 feet high with small, green-gray, linear leaves. Grows on dry plains and lower foothills, especially common in western Colorado. Blooms September-October.

Most of the better known composites have spreading rays—each of which is really a flower, though usually sterile—surrounding a disc of less conspicuous tubular flowers, these latter being normally the fertile ones Sunflowers are familiar examples. Throughout some genera of this great family, and in various species of additional genera, the rays are totally absent. Rabbit brush is one of the composites whose flower heads have no rays. They are showy only because so many of them cluster together, and because each small flower contributes a speck of bright gold. They are distinctly plants of desert lands, and in the fall season each big clump is a perfect mound of color. As winter nears, the color pales and fades, though flowers hang on a long time. Rabbit brush is not a sagebrush, even though both grow on the same dry plains and both are members of the composite family.

Composite Family

Easter Daisy, *Townsendia sericea,* Hook.

Flower heads, 2 inches across, are formed of about 30 white rays, slightly striated and indented at the tips, surrounding a disc, about ¾ inch in diameter, of numerous tubular gold-colored florets. Plant is about 3 inches high and carries one or several flower heads right on the top of a spreading tough root crown from which also rise numerous, narrow, linear leaves about 2-3 inches long. Grows on grassy plains, and foothills. Blooms April-May.

These are among the very earliest of the plains flowers. Their typical occurrence is as isolated plants, one here and one there between grass turfs in areas of rather tight prairie sod. They are so low and compact that they are not easy to find, even though their beauty well justifies the search. Spring has come when Easter daisies are out, even though the plains are still clad in winter gray with only a faint suggestion that in time the range will be green. Several other members of this daisylike genus are found in the foothills and plains. One of the commoner of these, *Townsendia eximia,* is easily distinguished by its short spreading branches which carry a few leaves.

Composite Family

Showy Fleabane, *Erigeron speciosus,* C. FONG

Flower head, 1½ inches across, is composed of about 200 narrow rays of brilliant lavender color, surrounding a button-like center ½ inch in diameter, of numerous, bright-gold, tubular florets packed closely together. Plant is 1½ to 3 feet high, freely branching, with numerous flower heads; leaves oblong or oval 2-3 inches long. Grows in shady places, rich moist soil, montane and sub-alpine zones. Blooms late July-September.

As the season advances, these aster-like flowers become the most conspicuous color notes in our high-altitude aspen groves. They come after early flowers are gone and bloom with a profusion unknown to most shade-loving plants. Before they too are gone a leaf here and there on the geranium plants in these same places will have turned bright red; on the ground, ivory colored puff-balls will be ready to discharge their clouds of brown spores, and the very first of the aspen leaves will have turned yellow and be drifting down. Showy fleabanes may linger to catch the first fall snows. Another of the many members of this genus, *Erigeron trifidus,* grows on the plains and brings out its small white blossoms in late April when it may catch the last spring snows.

Composite Family

Alpine Sunflower, *Hymenoxys grandiflora,* Parker

Flower head is 3 to 4 inches across, the central disk, an inch in diameter, made up of over a hundred tiny, tubular, golden florets, surrounded by about 30 bright yellow rays which are flat and notched at the outer end. Plant is 5 to 15 inches tall of one or several woolly stems, with leaves divided into several narrow lobes. Grows on alpine slopes. June-July.

This woolly-stemmed, dwarf sunflower, sometimes called old-man-of-the-mountains, or sun-god, is a startling surprise for the newcomer to our above-timberline tundras. One expects smaller more timid flowers here, and so at first the big bright faces of these plants seem out of place. Then we come to love them for their gay defiance of tough growing conditions and think of them as the proper guardians of high windy places. Whole colonies of them will be found with all the flower heads faced in the same direction. This will be a direction from which they receive strong light, and is a form of heliotropism. The stems, however, do not twist through a full half circle each day to follow the sun.

COMPOSITE FAMILY

THISTLE, *Circium undulatum,* SPRENG.

    Flower heads, 1½ to 2 inches broad, are solitary at the ends of stems and branches, and made up of numerous (100 or more) rose-colored, tubular florets fluffing out widely at their tops and grouped tightly together at their bases into an involucre made of many little, overlapping green bracts. Plant is about 3 feet tall with gray-green deeply cut leaves; stem and leaf ribs armed with prickles. Grows on plains, extending into foothills. Blooms May-September.

    Thistles of some sort are found in all parts of Colorado. Above timberline they take on grotesque shapes. In one, high-altitude thistle, *Circium hookerianum,* the whole woolly top of the plant, formed of compressed leaves and inconspicuous flower heads, bends over to resemble the head and neck of some shaggy animal. In our sub-alpine hay meadows a different species, *Circium drummondii,* may spread flat on the ground with no main stem and keep its flower heads so low that the mowing machine goes right over it catching only tops of a few leaves. On the plains are other species with shaving-brush-like flower heads. In spite of the prickles on their leaves and stems, horses nip off the flower heads and eat them with relish. Donkeys and mules seem to like them even better.

CLASSIFICATION OF PLANTS

All plants are related to each other in the sense that every one of them is descended from a common primitive uni-cellular life form which came into existence on this planet millions of years ago. As the remote progeny of that ancestral cell, or group of cells, became scattered over the earth and faced diverse conditions, which in turn changed with the ages, these millions of related organisms exhibited profound changes such that the differences in form, size and structure have become more noticeable than are the badges of common inheritance. This is the process called Evolution. Changes are established so slowly, however, that the immediate descendants of any particular plant, or the offspring from cross-pollination within a closely related group, will continue for many generations to be substantially identical in structure with the parents. As long as substantial identity in structure exists, all of these individual plants form a single "species." As these species are discovered, botanists give each of them a Latin name. Within Colorado over 2000 such separate species of flowering plants are known. Minute variations such as color of petals or degree of hairness of leaf or stem are treated as "varieties" within the species.

Many thousands of these substantially identical plants may be found scattered over parts of a state, or over several states, or even throughout a life zone area comprising parts of several continents. Within the life zone favorable to them, the only geographical limits seem to be those affecting distribution of live seed.

In the search for plants, many different species are found, either in the same or more often in different localities, in which the resemblances are close; in fact many parts are almost identical, but persistent differences are also present. A common ancestor several hundred or several thousand years back may have existed, but evolutionary changes have brought notice-able differences in the respective descendant groups. If the changes are not too great, especially if the mechanisms of reproduction have not been so greatly changed as to make cross-pollination totally impossible between plants of the several species, these related species, wherever they may have been found, are said to comprise a "genus." To this, also, a Latin name is given. *Lillium,* for example, is the generic name of all true lilies everywhere; *umbellatum,* however, is the specific name of the group to which our Colo-rado mountain lily belongs; and *"Lillium umbellatum"* is the full name of the plant shown on page 10.

Still greater differences in plant and flower structure are found, coupled, however, with strong resemblances in significant parts of the structure. This has led to grouping a considerable number of genera together into a "family." Latin names also are given to the families. For these names there are, in most cases, well established English equivalents which we have used here without repeating the more technical family name. Within each family all genera and each species of every genus will exhibit strong resemblances in the mechanism of seed production, and the general pattern of the organs of reproduction will be recognizably similar. For example, all species in the rose family (with very few exceptions) have numerous stamens arranged in whorls; they also have a calyx formed of five sepals joined together at the base.

Other groupings, such as "Orders" comprised of several families, or "tribes" composed of several genera within a family, are used by botanists, but for the purposes of this booklet we have used only the names of families, genera and species.

To the amateur one of the most interesting phases of plant classification is the way in which, as we pass from one life zone to another, or from one part of the state to another part within the same life zone, we find that a plant species which we have observed at one spot, is replaced, at another, by a different species within the same genus. We find our white mariposa, *Calochortus gunnisonii,* on the east side of the mountains, then, in flat clay plains in southwestern Colorado, we find the sego lily, *Calochortus nuttallii,* which is a similar, but quite distinct mariposa with cream-colored petals and a crooked, much shorter stem. Beyond the boundaries of Colorado numerous other species of *Calochortus* are found, all of them different from ours, but all of them quite obviously mariposas.

HOW PLANT POPULATIONS MAINTAIN THEMSELVES AND SPREAD

Infant mortality is high and life expectancy short among the flowering plants. They not only struggle against extremes of climate, but they are the primary food of the animal kingdom, and so pursued by creatures that have the advantages of sight and locomotion. It is only by marvelous fecundity and by ingenious devices for seed dispersal that plants maintain their position on the earth.

The first objective of every plant is to produce fertile seed in as large a quantity as the supplies of food and moisture and the length of season will permit. Pollination, which brings about the merging of the male and female cells, is essential to seed production. The majority of plants combine in a single flower stamens which carry in anthers on their tips the male element pollen and one or more pistils which hold at their base ovaries containing the female cells. These ovaries are reached by the pollen through the style and the stigma at its tip. The flower may thus fertilize itself in most species, but cross-pollination from other plants of the same species makes for more vigorous stock. The showy petals and petal-like sepals, which draw our eyes to flowers, make the flower conspicuous also to bees, moths, and even birds which act as pollen bearers. Other lures to this same end are fragrances and nectar. The detailed mechanisms by which the various plants increase the likelihood of cross-fertilization, within the brief period that any given set of cells is capable of fertilization, are numerous indeed and a fascinating study.

In most plants, seed develops and becomes fully ripe in a matter of weeks after fertilization has occurred. It is also commonplace for a single flower to produce a seed pod or other fruit which may contain hundreds of separate perfect seeds.

The next step is to scatter this seed over an area wide enough to reduce the risk of all of them perishing at once, and also wide enough to keep the survivors from competing too closely with each other for soil, moisture and sunlight. Here again fascinating devices come into play. Building each seed with a plume or bit of fluff at its tip so that it can be carried far by wind, is one of the commonest tricks. Other seeds float easily on water and so reach new sites. Other seeds invite being eaten by birds or beasts, and depend upon a fraction of them either being carelessly dropped before being swallowed, or having tough enough shells to resist digestion. Quite a number of plants produce seed pods which, when they become thoroughly dry split open with a jerk flipping seeds over distances of several feet. Finally there are the various burs and barbed seeds that are carried for miles by animals and by man.

Seeds thus become scattered over the earth, and so numerous and efficient are the devices of dispersion that in the course of years the seeds from a single plant colony, and from the successive new outlying colonies it founds, may become spread over miles of distance. Only a few barriers completely stop such spreading. Oceans, high mountains and broad deserts are the most effective barriers, but even they do not always stop every seed of every plant.

This spread of seeds pays little attention to life zone limits, or to such interference as rivers, hills or local barren areas may present. Over and past all of such minor obstacles the flow of seed rolls.

The final problem for the seed is how to germinate and become established in the place it lands. If that place is totally unsuitable for the particular species, the answer there is failure. Many seeds may invade a locality too dry for their development. In such a case, even if germination occurs, all such seedlings will die before a single plant matures. Heavy frost may act as a like absolute veto to other seedlings that venture too high in altitude or too far north in latitude for their own limitations. By forces such as these, each species of plant stays contained within limits beyond which it cannot become established, even though individual seeds may in great numbers invade impossible localities.

Mature plants may tolerate conditions which wipe out all tender seedlings of the same species. This leads to interesting patterns of plant distribution in semi-desert areas, such as occur in parts of Colorado. Once or twice in a century a series of two, three, or even five successive years may occur when the soil is moist and extraordinarily favorable to plant growth throughout weeks or months of the spring and summer. In these special times seeds that have invaded a usually hostile area may, if they have retained fertility, germinate, push their roots deep, and become so vigorous that when normal dry years follow these particular plants live on and thrive for the remainder of their lives, even though their own seeds fall on barren ground and the species maintains only a precarious or temporary foothold in the area.

Governed by forces such as these, and limited by competition with each other, plant species have for ages taken their places in the global economy and carried out their part of the commandment to be fruitful and multiply. Otherwise we and the animals we prey upon could not exist.

FLOWER PATTERNS

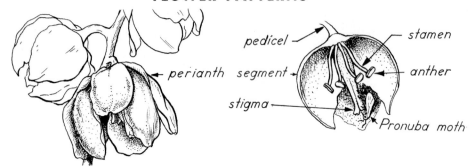

YUCCA: has six perianth segments, six stamens and a pistil with 3 divisions.

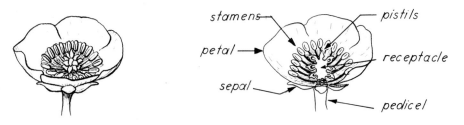

BUTTERCUP: is made up of separate petals, many stamens and several pistils.

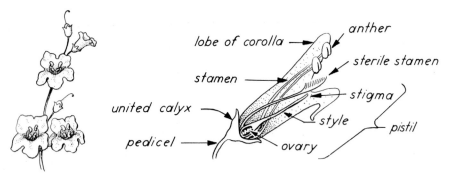

PENSTEMON: has a united, irregular corolla with few stamens and one pistil.

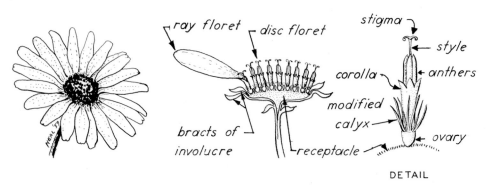

DETAIL

COMPOSITE: many individual flowers are closely packed together, surrounded by an involucre.

PLANT PARTS

INFLORESCENCE: refers to the way the flowering area of a plant is arranged.

A spike: flowers are attached directly to a stalk.

A raceme: similar to a spike, but each flower is attached to the flowering stalk by a pedicel.

pedicel

pedicel

An umbel: an umbrella-like form of inflorescence in which a cluster of pedicels all arise from one point at the head of a flowering stalk.

STEMS: the stem is that part of the plant from which roots, buds, and flowers arise.

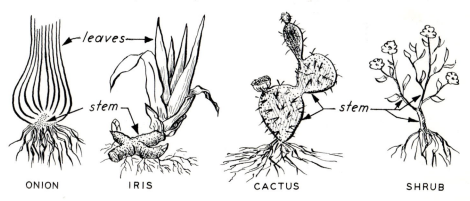

leaves

stem

stem

ONION IRIS CACTUS SHRUB

ROOTS: absorb moisture and minerals for the plant from the soil, and provide storage.

FIBROUS ROOT TAP ROOT

LEAF SHAPES, ARRANGEMENTS, and PARTS

SHAPES

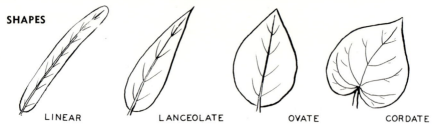

LINEAR LANCEOLATE OVATE CORDATE

SIMPLE leaves: the blade consists of a single segment.

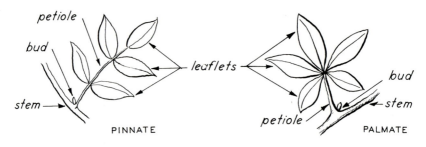

PINNATE PALMATE

COMPOUND leaves: the blade is divided into several leaflets.

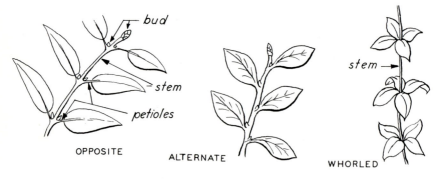

OPPOSITE ALTERNATE WHORLED

ARRANGEMENTS of leaves on their stems.

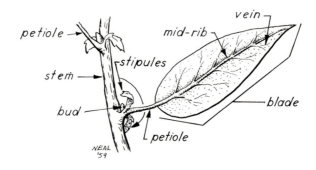

NEAL '59

PARTS of an idealized simple leaf.

INDEX

Available from Publications Department
Denver Museum of Natural History
City Park, Denver, Colorado 80205